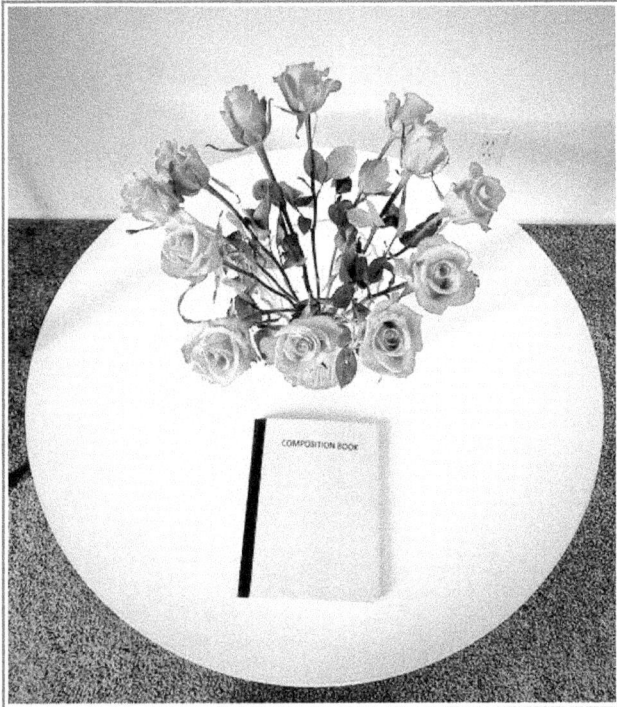

Poems Before Breakfast
Poetic Micro Essays

This is an autobiographical work.

ISBN: 978-1-7338478-7-2 (trade paperback)

Published by Falcon West Books, First Edition, 2023

10 9 8 7 6 5 4 3 2 1

Printed in the United States of America.

Cover design: Eve West Bessier

Other Falcon West Books by Eve West Bessier

New Rain, a visionary novel (2005)
Roots Music: Listening to Jazz (2019)
Exposures: Tripod Poems (2020)
In the Flow of Grace (2020)
Pink Cadillacs: Short Stories (2021)

Poems Before Breakfast

Poetic Micro Essays

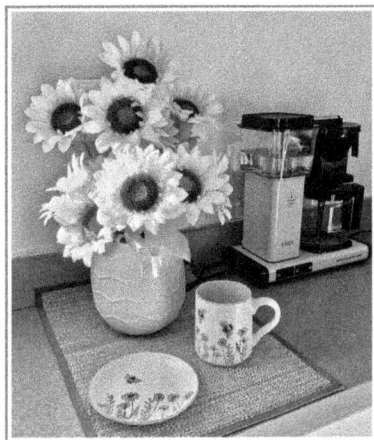

Eve West Bessier

Falcon West Books

For Pat and Elisabeth
who listened to me read
each of these poems,
written before breakfast
and shared afterwards.

Author's Note and Acknowledgments

These poems were first published as a personal
daily online blog from mid-January through
mid-April of 2023.

The response to the blog was so enthusiastic that
I decided to gather the poems into a collection
and make them available in book form.

I hope that you will hold them in your hands
and in your heart.

Several poems from this collection are also published in
the following online journals:

Writing in a Woman's Voice
Southwest Word Fiesta
The Journal of Radical Wonder

Introduction

As a daily spiritual practice, I wrote a poem every morning before breakfast for three months in 2023.

The resulting poems reveal my process of healing through the collective trauma of the pandemic and my personal challenge of living out of a suitcase for nine months while searching for a place to live, and winding up in an unexpected new hometown.

Each of these poems is a rendering of deeply personal experience, a brief philosophical treatise, a candid self-revelation. As such, they are micro essays written in poetic language.

For two decades now, I've enjoyed writing in a form I created called, *Tripod Poems.* I pick three words by randomly opening a dictionary and seeing where my right thumb lands. The three random words become the title of the poem, are contained within the poem, and through their often odd juxtaposition, bring forth unexpected insight.

I hope you will enjoy these *Poems Before Breakfast,* though you may read them at any time, of course!

Note: I sometimes use a Spanish language dictionary. Some dictionary listings contain dual words, ie: trade wind.

Table of Contents

Oaxacan carved jackrabbit

These poems are a gift from my heart

Day 1

Exhale - Progress - Drunk

So much loss to release,

the leaden detritus
after the deluge,

the beaten debris
after the tsunami.

Certainly, a storm surge
is what we've all survived
in these fear-filled years.

Exhale this searing pain.
Inhale a taste of faith.

Make progress in baby steps,
delicate mendings of nets,
incremental movements
toward a healing wholeness.

Life exists, persists with
the transition from inhale
to exhale, to inhale, to exhale.

Can we dream again
of being drunk on life!

Day 2

Guideline - Untold - Panache

Where do I place the focus
of my attention?

It's all about perspective,
or so they say.

Not just the facts, Ma'am.

Give me the context, subtext,
a hyperlink to the untold.

How do I unfold
the topographical map
that holds the guidelines
for safe routes,
low passes through treacherous peaks,
high roads through valleys
swollen with flood?

How do I trespass
into the unknown Self,

and do it with some panache?

Day 3

Candle Wick - Gird - Stopgap

Without a candle wick,
wax won't adorn the darkness
with that sweet, soft light
we now call forth
mostly for romance.

Before Edison,
that mellow glow
lit the whole world
for millennia.

When electricity fails us,
candle wicks become our stopgap,
illuminating our darkness.

The wax which girds
the slowly burning wick,
melts away in the light play
of a self-annihilating duet.

What wick and wax
conjure my internal light
when a dark night
of the soul descends?

Day 4

Simmer - Doubt - Galvanize

I utilized a crockpot
for the first time yesterday.

Such luxury,
letting dinner simmer
while we were out listening
to a friend read her poetry.

Then all of us coming home
to a sumptuous meal at the ready.

Why do I always cast doubt
upon outcomes,
not trusting situations,
connections to galvanize
exactly as required?

Serendipity and synchronicity
reliably come through for me,

so why not let life simmer
with flavors maturing naturally,
until a welcomed feast is served?

Day 5

Disburden - Shanghaied - Bathe

It was common enough practice
to rapidly become metaphor.

Aren't we all *Shanghaied* into this life,
burdened with an unknown purpose?

Aren't we all not so much guests
as servants aboard ship, tricked into
thinking we are meant to take the helm,
when the compass spins and trade winds
fill our sails at their own whim.

Free will being debatable,
we still fly all manner of banners
on the masthead claiming our dominion.

Were we instead, in the unfettered
sea air, to bathe in the brisk balm
of a lithe acquiescence,

our bondage might be broken,
the deadweight albatross released
from the lariat around our necks,
our souls then disburdened of the need
to control our own destinies.

Day 6

Tickle - Note - Frank

There's a tickle
at back of my
subconscious

a slight shimmer
a glitter in the wind

a foretaste
of delight

Like a school child
passing a secret note

my heart extends
an invitation

a love letter
a Valentine

to be open and
generously frank

to fill unabashedly
with glee

Day 7

Ballast - Self-pollination - Hunch

I feel heavily tethered,
survival saps my energy.

After all this self-pollination
to keep flowering
despite obstacles,
and unfavorable odds,

I am ready to receive
the blessing of bees!

Accessible weight
is essential
to the controlled ascent
of hot air balloons,

and also, it seems,
to spiritual attunement.

I have an urgent hunch
it's time to hoist
the sandbags overboard,

to release
the ballast of grief.

Day 8

Distinguish - Truth Serum - Dampen

I woke up dull,
a contradiction in terms,
to be sure.

If only there were
a truth serum
I could self-administer
to determine
my ultimate purpose.

This dark morning dampens
my enthusiasm,
withers my zeal,
leaves me feeling weary.

I've tried so diligently
all these years
to distinguish
which path to follow,
which road not to take,

and how it can make
all the difference.

Day 9

Hibernate - Polite - Awkward

Winter in an untried environment.
All I desire is to hibernate.

Knowing no one, I miss being polite.

Miss the occasional small talk,
the awkward laughter.

Seeing people smile
is a simple luxury
we haven't experienced
for a long while
behind our white K-95s.

I dream of water,
of wanting to wade out
into lake stillness.

Instead, I float oarless
in a wooden row boat,

reaching for reflected light,
for green water on my fingertips,

waiting to awaken.

Day 10

Sensuous - Daybed - Kiss

I gave away my red daybed.
No room in the moving truck.
No place for it in the new house.

Nine months of an unsure future,
of being afraid for my long-term safety
did not provide the kind of leisure
that leads to sensuous daydreams.

There are so many lovely things
I've had to kiss goodbye,
last-minute, over the past eight years
to get from all of those theres,
to my brand new here.

I know, this isn't where
you want the poem to go
with these hard-to-believe random
words that seem so perfect
for a tender love song.

It's too early in the morning
for something more like soft porn.

Okay. If you insist.

A Rococo, late Baroque sky
comes to mind, the kind
with chubby cherubim
and pink wisps of white cloud
in arabesque over cornflower blue.

Down below,
rests an unclad female figure
reclined on a sumptuous daybed
of red velvet with a myriad
of rose embroidered pillows.

Her left arm extends upwards,
waves of amber hair falling
over porcelain shoulders.

Her right arm supports
her form on a pale elbow.

Behind her, sheer
lavender draperies
waft in a slight breeze,
while white cherry blossoms
float in gilded light.

One wayward blossom
touches down,
lands just so,
to kiss her,
just there.

Day 11

Contentment - Notwithstanding - Trifling

In my native language, *Nederlands*,
there are many compound words,
long strings of smaller words knit
together without benefit of hyphens
to create a furthering collective meaning.

In English, we have only a few of these.
Notwithstanding and nonetheless
being my favorites, not only
for their weirdness and odd looks,
but also for their philosophical meanings.

Both compressed word strings
express a rich Buddhist concept
for achieving contentment:
to be at peace despite circumstances,
to accept what is with grace,
no matter what might be
considered a better outcome.

No trifling matter!

Day 12

Flyleaf - Mystery - Holistic

The blank page
at the front and rear
of a published book
is called a flyleaf.

Perhaps to conjure
the concept that everything
begins and ends in emptiness.

To remind us as well,
that we all start
as a blank page,
and once we are gone,
our page will be blank again.

Even when the many pages
between our start and finish
are filled with every mystery
we've solved, and resonate
with all of our holistic selves,

that final sheet,
a mystic shroud,
is still the blank page,
the flyleaf
in the cosmic breeze.

Day 13

Hourglass - Chatter - Vine

An ornate brass hourglass
stands on the small round table
by the tall oval window.

Sand is still sifting
through the narrow portal,
but has mostly settled
in the lower vestibule.

All about the Victorian house
idle chatter resonates
as the evening's soiree
winds to a late closure.

Sophia sits on the sofa,
gazing at the vine pattern
of the over-stuffed cushions,
running her aged fingers
over the linen fabric.

Then, she slowly stands,
waddles to the window,
turns over the hourglass
just as only a few last
grains remain.

She pulls aside the lace curtain
to watch the guests depart,
below on the circular drive.

Final tufts of laughter rise
like startled doves,
in the stillness of night.

Day 14

Drought - Trade Wind - Beachcomber

Maui in deep drought.
Not a breath of trade wind.
102º in the shade.

The golden sand
a furnace underfoot,
discourages being
a beachcomber.

I dash into the water,
splash around, get eye-to-eye
with Hawaii's state fish,
the humuhumunukunukuāpuaʻa,
then dash back to my spot
under the wild acacias,
behind a pile of broken coral,
my private hideaway.

Inside my rental in Kihei,
with no air-conditioning,
is too stiflingly hot to sleep.

The airline lost my luggage.
What I do have with me,
was stolen in the rental car
break-in, even my driver's license.

No transportation
until a temporary
arrives days later.

I wander listlessly
in the open-air lobby
of the Hyatt Wailea,
where I am definitely not
a paying guest, just a refugee
from the heat and humidity.

In the evening, I swim all alone
in the hotel's huge circular pool,
with a tiled red hibiscus,
emulating art from Atlantis,
blooming underneath cool water.

Serene under moon gleam,
don't judge me, we are all
trying to survive this blistering,
relentless October heat.

The next morning, I spot dolphins
off the beach past the lava fields.

I paddle out with my snorkel,
fins and Boogie board.

I call to them.

They race toward me
at such velocity
it scares me.

Perhaps sensing my fear,
they race away.

I turn to see the shore
is way too far away from me.
I may be heading out to sea
in this deep current.

I paddle sideways along the shoreline
looking for a break in the riptide.

With constant kicking, I make it back
to the rocky beach, exhausted in safety.

It's been over twenty years now.
I have not yet returned to Maui,
though I long for her every so often.

Strange, the pull of that island,
like a siren song.

Red hibiscus for my hair.
Vibrant colors like nowhere else.
Scent of plumeria in the air.

Day 15

Conciliate - Herculean - Alacrity

To be of one mind,
even when it is only my own,
is a Herculean task.

Free-ranging ideas
running amok.
Random thoughts
pecking away at my brain.
Uninvited emotions
firing my synaptic wiring.

How do I conciliate
these diverse needs,
often opposite desires,
pesky tugs of war
that leave me worn out
from internal contradictions?

What I seek is alacrity,
smooth sailing
with clear direction.

Meanwhile,
I'll keep tacking
into the wind, toward
the nearest open shore.

Day 16

Instead - Possible - Compulsion

The desire
to have *that*

instead of *this*

is what haunts

what keeps happiness
always at bay

Betrays faith
that all is well
in this precious
intimate moment

The possible
is not always
a worthy goal

It can be an endless
grail journey

Why this compulsion
to reach elsewhere?

To find what appears

to be missing

To long for the
elusive *that*

instead of embracing
the present *this,*

when after
all the smoke
and mirrors

this is it

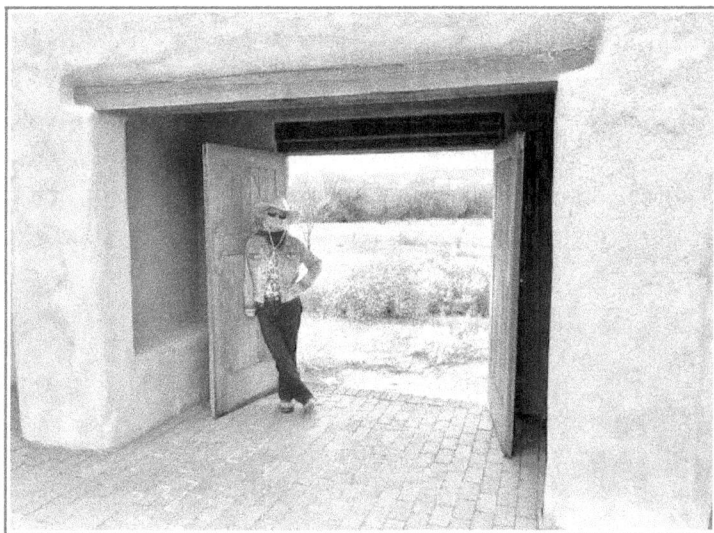

At Mesilla Valley Bosque State Park, Las Cruces

Day 17:

Shorebird - Essential - Accord

Sandpipers in early light,
narrow legs racing
to the receding hiss of surf,

thin black beaks
pecking sand
to seek beneath
for tiny nourishment.

Suddenly, they turn
all at once to outrun an
incoming rush of salt water
topped with sea foam.

A shorebird's morning
is rhythmic movement,
forth and back, forth and back,
a pattern of warp and woof
to weave the world.

To be in accord
with constant change,
essential letting go,
is to know nothing
is permanent, no wave
stays ashore.

Day 18

Douglas Fir - Grace - Ukulele

I've traded daily communion
with ponderosa pine

for occasional conversation
with Douglas fir.

I'm stumbling
with confused feet
over unknown terrain,

attempting grace,
still falling short.

What did Yoda say?
"Do, or do not. There is no try."

I'm trying way too hard.

Yielding to what is,
with no whimpered complaints,
may be the remedy.

Bring me the sweet strains
of a koa wood ukulele.
I need some unhurried,
calming aloha today.

Day 19

Graft - Tug - Facade

Our lives together
create a graft.

The weaknesses
in each of us
balanced by our
complementary strengths.

Just like two trees sharing
their genetic properties.

One being naturally selected
for greater height, the other
for firmer bark and larger girth,

grafted with each other,
they grow taller and stronger.

One is drought-resistant,
the other wards off molds.

One produces ample fruits,
the other builds resilient roots.

Each of our individual talents
are slowly woven together

to formulate an intricate pattern
of beauty and usefulness,
like a sweetgrass braided basket.

All initial tugs of war
between our needs and desires
slowly dissolve into a more
unified vision and joint purpose.

Eventually,
we are so safe together,
we can afford
to drop all facades,

each flowering
in complete authenticity,

each reaching
for the highest probability
of joy and meaning,

while never losing
our unique attributes.

Our relationship
is a grafting
of ever expanding
compassionate love.

Day 20

Sequester - Dictate - Offstage

I've learned it suits me to sequester.

Yes, the happiness experts insist
that interaction with others
for several hours a day
is essential, even for those
who are naturally introverts.

I can see how being a complete hermit
would deplete one's social skills,
make one estranged, skittish, even afraid.

Still, I will not allow the lab coats
on the happiness circuit
to dictate my daily dose
of the social three-ring circus.

It can be overwhelming.

All of those other psyches,
dancing bears, acrobats,
fire breathers, clowns
and shouting ring masters.

Being offstage is a relief,
feels like a new freedom.

So, for the moment,
I'll abide in the wings,

until I find enough need
to muster some courage
and go out to mingle.

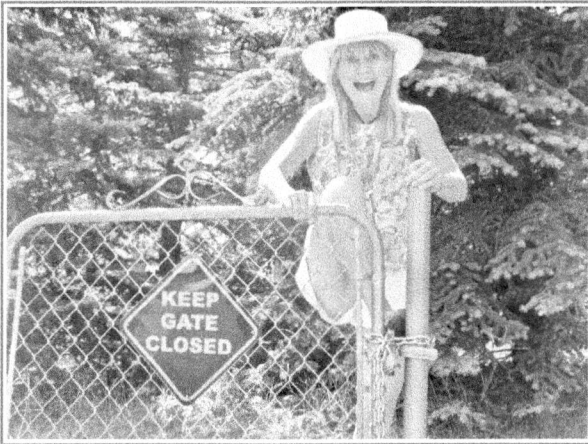

A locked gate with no fence in Evergreen, Colorado

Day 21

Dwell - Polite - Expend

Yesterday, on my way home,
a hefty black SUV
was driving on the opposite
side of the street towards me.

It appeared to be a police vehicle,
but as it passed, I saw white writing
on the side which read, *Polite.*

A shuttle of some sort,
I presume, but *Polite*
could be the motto
of my odd new home town.

At four-way stop signs,
it takes a while to go through,
as all of the drivers insist,
"Please, *you* go first."

That's not a prevalent attitude
in our *Me First* world.

It feels like we dwell
in the past here,
but in a good way,

in the 1970s, at a slower,
more generous pace.

People are aware
of each other's needs.

There is eye contact
and conversation in stores.
Comments on the weather,
apologies for being in the way.

No-one seems eager
to run over your feet
with their shopping cart,
or to compete for the fastest
moving check-out line.

The mindset here appears to be,
it's worth the extra time
to expend a little kindness,
to make a friend of a stranger.

There is considerable value in that,
and it's seriously contagious.

I find myself a bit perplexed
by all this unexpected courtesy,
but I will happily get used to it!

Day 22

Pocket - Incognito - Footloose

The jazz greats say,
when a tune plays just so,
that it is *in the pocket.*

Casino Royale high rollers
in Bond films flaunt
their tuxedo's deep pockets.

What's in our pockets?

Invisible currencies
racing through digital signals,
transferred by satellite
from our cellphones,
which hold the key
to our social visibility
and our access to money.

When you've got too much dough
in your Zen of Money dojo though,

better go incognito
if you want to be
footloose and free
from the instagram paparazzi.

To get your brand in key,
better lean mean
into the influencer scene
and spend it to trend it.

From what I've seen,
that's not my dream!

Doorway in Mesilla, New Mexico

Day 23

Redeem - Homecoming - Psalm

Can we redeem
our investments in love,
even the ones
that sapped us,
never feeding us?

Are all of our efforts
toward affection
and gentle empathy
eventually rewarded,
like a long-term bond
paid with interest accrued?

Or do we lose
our tender capital
when we love
without reciprocation,
when we love a narcissist,
someone incapable
of feeling for us,
or revealing to us
their true selves?

When our heart's account
is fully drained
and nothing remains

but a debt of sorrow,
there must be
a homecoming then.

A prodigal daughter
returning, after a long
journey of giving
to no avail
what should be
greatly honored.

This is a psalm
for all the love songs
sung yet never received,
for genuine affection
gone unappreciated.

This is a balm to heal all
of our unfruitful investments.

Let us choose now
to love ourselves better,
to secure stronger stock
in which to harbor
the trust funds
of our generous hearts.

Day 24

Downbeat - Own - Sameness

I'm looking for
a downbeat,

watching for a signal
from an invisible
conductor,

listening for
those three taps
of the baton.

Perhaps,

I could own
this restart, throw
a few pick-up notes
ahead of the bar.

Maybe even
a graceful run
to shake up
the sameness,

although there is security
in predictability for me.

In this new reality,
safety is essential
to my well-being.

It would be freeing
to at least know
the key signature.

I'm hoping for G major,
a warm vocal range.

Then again, *All Blues*,
by Miles Davis,
one of my favorites, turns
G major into a cool key.

So, no guarantee
the tune would be gleeful.

Maybe just a touch
of melancholy?

Surely, not a waltz,
unless it's in 6/8,
with that funky
West African
syncopated gait.

Let the tempo start slow,
a mellow adagio,

then it could grow
into a more upbeat flow,
maybe even into allegretto.

Vivace is too fast
to handle today.

In any case,
I'll get myself tuned,
run through some scales,
a few arpeggios,

so that when
the maestro's
baton lifts,

I'll be prepped
for the downbeat.

Day 25

Cairn - Potent - Flume

In Hawaii, rock cairn altars are called ahu.

Stacks of black lava ahu
lead across uneven flows
toward the coast, where
translucent flumes
of turquoise light-infused
ocean waves shoot
through jagged cliffs
from hidden carved
caves far below.

Like geysers rising,
with unpredictable timing,
each incoming wave compresses
into smaller, tighter spaces
until the pressure is so potent
water explodes upwards,

rushes skyward
into tropical brilliance
with mesmerizing
prismatic fireworks
that hiss to cool hot lava
with a rainbow mist
of salty kisses.

Day 26

Misty - Cycle - Humble

Grey overcast softens
the mid-winter sunrise.

Down below, the White Sands
are shrouded in moisture
as their gypsum slowly releases
its dampness, low temperatures
rising with each slight gain
in solar radiation.

I feel humble in this grey space,
aware of my minuteness
in the overall scheme.

Amid these grand complexities
in the cycle of a turning world,
I am a mere mote in a frail sunbeam.

In this mellowing moment,
I am neither ambitious
nor on purpose,
simply unclear
like the weather.

I settle gently
into these muted hours,

while mourning doves
coo their plaintive calls
from nearby trees
and neighboring rooftops.

The subdued light soothes,
and sun-lover though I be,
this misty morning
strangely suits me.

Day 27

Nip - Shield - Dip

To dip ourselves,
like Achilles,
hero of grief and distress,
in the River Styx,

in order to become
invulnerable,

except, of course,

for that pesky ankle,
that unavoidable point
of human fault and foible,

where Cerberus,
that heinous
three-headed canine,
can nip at our naked heel,
even at the gates to Hades.

No mystic river
can shield us
from the fires
of grief and distress.

They speed the crucible
that leads to healing.

It is our hero's journey
to emancipate growth
from our own
tortured mythologies.

Day 28

Flurry - Pent - Unsheathe

Why do I believe
in such a diminutive way?

When I was a seventh-grader,
I was taller than all of the boys.

I played center on the girls
basketball team.

All of my early tallness
perturbed me.

Being so far ahead of the curve,
having an adult body as a pre-teen,
reaching fertility at age eight,
made me want to hide away.

I wanted to be tiny and skinny
like my prepubescent cohorts.

These days, all but a few
of my male and female friends
are taller and larger me,
yet I still feel strangely
immense in mixed company.

I'd like to finally
release my capacity
in some productive flurry
of pent up tallness.

To rise confidently
out of the bulrushes,
like a great blue heron
taking wing and ascending
into an expanse of open sky.

I long to no longer
want to be small,
to no longer fear
any form of largeness.

I long to unsheathe
and wield my spiritual
warrior's sword of words
like an intrepid samurai.

And perhaps swish
a few long shots
through the hoop
with a satisfying swoosh!

Day 29

Embroider - Recover - Consistency

As a child, I liked to embroider,
a common hobby then,
like painting by numbers,
knitting and crocheting.

I still own a pillow I embroidered
at maybe age ten, depicting
that Americana darling, Holly Hobby,
wearing her outsized prairie bonnet,
embellished with colored yarns.

I have yet to recover the pillow
since moving, but I know
it's in box 109, still not unpacked,
waiting patiently in the garage.

I may not display
that needlework today,
but it serves to distill
the consistency of my journey.

If that little pillow still exists,
with its splashes of piebald hues,
I too must have existed then,
as a real child, needle in hand,

not just as a faint ghost
of a distant memory.

Having tangible things
from the past, helps us
embroider our personal
histories, keeps us connected
to the easily unraveled
threads of time and memory.

After writing this poem,
I went to the garage.
I found box 109, and pulled
little Holly Hobby
from her dark confines.

She now rests on my bed
to honor the innocent
and multi-talented child
I was then, and am still.

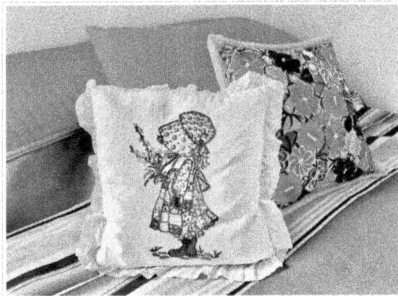

Day 30

Jacaranda - Script - Hurtle

Why do I hurtle myself
so vehemently
into the future?

Improvising is fine
for jazz, for dance
and occasional poetry.

For creating a life,
it's risky.

Mind you,
I've mostly had
no choice in the matter.

In order to avoid
rip currents at high tides,
I've had to swim sideways,
parallel to shore,
looking for a safe way
back to terra firma.

Survival requires
fast reflexes,
accurate timing,

an art of improvisation
in each moment.

I still love to wear
my favorite surf skirt
from *Rip Curl Girl*,
bought decades ago
in sunny San Diego,
that lovely city of amethyst
blooming jacaranda trees
and cooling ocean breezes.

But that doesn't mean
I want to ride big surf,
or even keep improvising
out of sheer necessity.

I'm so ready
to write my own script,
or at least be promoted
to junior editor.

I'm not clueless
as to the presence
of a higher power
holding the fountain pen,
I just think it's high time
to give me that red pencil!

Day 31

Turnabout - Nourish - Frankincense

In Old City Jerusalem,
inside the sanctified center
of the domed Church
of the Holy Sepulcher,

the site of Christ's tomb
holding the Stone of Unction,
where his body was laid
and anointed after
his brutal crucifixion,

a gold-plated ornate bowl,
known as a thurible, slowly
swings overhead, back and forth.

Hanging from a chain
perhaps forty feet long,
the thurible makes
a majestic arch
over the mosaic floor
of the darkened chapel.

It is kept in constant motion
by a Greek Orthodox priest
in somber cassock tugging
on a long, knotted rope.

The censer vessel,
filled with burning
myrrh and frankincense,
sways overhead,
trailing blue smoke
that scents the heavy space
with the pungent odor
of centuries-old adoration.

It is a smell I know well
from my Catholic upbringing.

It is a low-hanging,
dense, regal fog
that might have made
the infant Jesus sneeze
when brought as healing
gift in a censer by Balthazar,
one of the three Magi.

Frankincense has medicinal
properties and is known
to also nourish the soul,
removing impurities.

Standing inside the weight
of this cathedral's history,
with the thick incense wafting
from wall to formidable wall,
I try to stifle an irritable cough.

With each sweep
and every turnabout
at the top of its arch,
that momentary pause
before the next descent,
the censer vessel
is the pendulum
of an historical clock.

Jerusalem is a city
in which time becomes
multi-dimensional.

On one modern avenue
lined with new housing
made of old Jerusalem stone,
you are in the present. Then,
just around the next corner,
you pass into a narrow alley
and are dropped back
into the lap of the Byzantine.

Here, the future dream
and the shadows
of the deep past
undulate continuously.

Day 32

Engender - Sanguine - Furnish

Wishing to live in comfort
is a basic need, a desire
to seek pleasure over pain.

Nesting well is enjoyable.
We furnish our homes
with carefully chosen
chairs, rugs, couches, beds.

All of this effort
is meant to engender
a sanguine mood
in our personal sanctuaries.

Why not then furnish
our minds for equal comfort?

Clear away clutter.
Nurture supportive habits
of thought and action.

Relax on sofas of imagination
that engender a sanguine mood
to soothe and soften the sharp
corners of a hectic day.

Day 33

Practice - Hinder - Windbreak

Writing these *Tripod Poems*
is part of my morning practice.

For over two decades now,
I've turned to this original method
of urging poetry from random selection
to unearth hidden potentials
and render unusual perceptions.

I sometimes worry
the structured format
may hinder a more organic flow.

The random words act
as conduits for creative thought,
but do they possibly constrict
the conceptual direction
of these philosophical treatises?

I believe limits are essential
to any creative process.
Without them, it's hard to start,
and easy to become distracted.

When everything is possible,
few things are probable.

Currently,
writing these daily poems
provides a windbreak
in stormy weather.

It allows my tempest-tossed
thoughts to gently settle
on an elegant bench,

in the corner of a well-tended
Zen garden, facing a fountain
next to a tall bamboo fence,

where the wind is stilled.

Day 34

Retread - Literal - Fierce

Folk art upholds
traditional codes,
values, patterns,
long-traveled allegories
that create a collective
community-building
her story and his story.

Fine art can be fierce
in its focus to break down
traditional codes,
expose outmoded values,
eschew patterns
in order to not retread
the long-traveled roads
of myth and allegory.

Yet, fine art can erode
the connectivity that holds
together community,
seeing folk art as being
too literal a translation
of the world, fine art
can push the boundaries
of individuality too deeply
into narcissistic expression.

Is there a fertile middle
ground of creativity,
where we can explore
beauty and meaning
to build a bridge between
folk and fine?

Zuni Mountain Lion Fetish, charcoal drawing by Eve

Day 35

Paste - Entrance - Atmosphere

The motto for New Mexico
is, *Land of Enchantment.*

The moniker praises the state's
expansive, mesa-strewn views
that entrance the mind with beauty
and expand the soul's capacity
for greater understanding.

Such outrageous spaciousness
creates an atmosphere
of audacious possibility.

It can also gravely intimidate,
act as reminder of nature's ability
to quickly overwhelm any
individual or collective intention.

The tension between
the concrete and the divine
is palpable here, a feeling
that we might be able
to cut and paste ourselves
into this outsized landscape,
but we must work diligently
to belong here, to deserve

querencia, an innate relationship
with land and place.

New Mexico is not gentle.
However charming she may seem
in our romantic dreams,
she is a land of harsh extremes.

To thrive here, even to survive here,
requires a willingness to strip away
all conventional expectations
of comfort and security.

Here, the high-altitude sun sears.
The winter cold freeze-dries.
Relentless mountain lightning
sets massive forests afire.

Late summer monsoon rain
creates violent flash floods
in the dry lowlands, while
for the rest of the year,
water is a scarcity,
well-guarded in acequias,
or only present in the long
memories of dried arroyos.

Golden eagles soar overhead,
while ravens caw and cut corners
under white wisps of striated cloud.

Coyotes howl at pink-hued moons.

Rattlesnakes coil beneath
jagged outcroppings.

Ancient petroglyphs
are carved on the dark
surface of volcanic rocks.

Pueblo dancers in buffalo
headdresses step gently
to the thunderous drumming
of their sacred ceremonies.

And the sky, the sky, the sky!
Unending, azure, majestic,
with low-riding storm clouds
close enough to almost touch.

Then comes the spring wind.
The wind, the wind, the wind!

It invades every nook and cranny,
coats absolutely everything
with the fine, white dust
of the high desert's
Pleistocene skin.

View of the Sacramento Mountains from Three Rivers Petroglyphs

Day 36

Songbird - Mat - Disillusion

I woke up this morning
to the elaborate vocal patterns
of a songbird near my window.

An early arrived robin,
always a harbinger of spring,
was welcoming the sunrise.

I admire the optimism
as inclement weather
has not yet finished
moving through.

The willows in the park
are slowly leafing in,
despite a cold wind
and flakes of snow.

Spring begins
before it is fully seen.

Our own progress
can be equally stealthy.

Life has called me to the mat,
and I've come to the challenge

like a prize-fighter, with fists
of resistance at the ready.

Perhaps that was a snap
judgement, a miscalculation
of what is required
for the task at hand,
which may be the need

to embrace disillusion,
a word so often misconstrued.
The definition is, "to leave
without illusion or naive faith."

Why then does disillusion*ed,*
just a tiny suffix added,
mean, "to be disappointed
or dissatisfied?"

Such an odd shift in meaning.

Are we disappointed
when we let go of our illusions
and our blind faith?

What does it say
about our culture
that satisfaction
is based on maintaining

our illusions?

Let my faith be
mature, not naive,

and let me approach
the mat anew, this time
like a gymnast, or a yogi,

without illusions.

Day 37

Tenebrous - Lenitive - Plethora

Tenebrous! Tenebrous! Tenebrous!

A spell to cast away
the gloom, making room
for generous illumination!

Lenitive! Lenitive! Lenitive!

A prayer for deep healing,
a sweet balm to cure
the wounds of disillusion!

Plethora! Plethora! Plethora!

An invocation to plenty,
a name well worthy
of a lesser-known goddess,
guardian of the ample harvest!

Tenebrous! Lenitive! Plethora!

Tenebrous! Lenitive! Plethora!

Tenebrous! Lenitive! Plethora!

Day 38

Intention - Instrumental - Cyclamen

My opa and oma's house,
was one-third of a two-story triplex,
made of stoic red brick,
as are most houses in Holland.

I was born there, downstairs,
though for decades I thought
I was born in the tiny
upstairs bedroom with only
a porthole window, high up
in the front-facing wall.

Memory is a fickle witness,
too easily swayed by emotion,
a faulty faculty that fades over time.

Did my oma love cyclamen?
I remember her dining room
always having one in bloom
on the table in a ceramic pot.

Related to the primrose,
the white or lavender-tinted
blossoms are imbedded
in my childhood memory.

Is recalling the past
instrumental to anything?

They say that those
who do not know history
are doomed to repeat it.

But do we not always have choices?

There is certainly a sinister repetition
of grave errors and heinous crimes
in our collective species story.

Are these not more likely
the result of political powers
squelching our societal development
for greed, profit and elite control?

The criminal, they say,
always returns to the scene
of the crime.

This leads me to believe
that he or she not only
remembers perfectly
the scheme of wrong doing,
but even revels in it.

They also say that action
follows intention.

So, maybe too much focus
on past faults and fractures
supports repeated future failure.

Then there is the ugly issue
of falsely depicting history,
of outright sabotage to erase
those heinous crimes from record,
in order to believe in the lie that
the blood-stained slates are clean.

How does an innocent memory
of blooming cyclamen on my
oma's dining room table
invoke such deep questioning?

Everything is connected.

My shaken opa and oma held
their three frightened children,
including my then nine-year-old
mother, while sequestered beneath
that same sturdy table
during countless Nazi air raids.

That same simple brick house
was invaded by Nazi soldiers.

I'm certain no cyclamen
was blooming then.

Day 39

Stunning - Linger - Fledge

Three things are needed
to leave the nest: muscle,
feathers, fearlessness.

It's a long way down
if you should fall,
but an endless sky awaits.

The wind is willing,
the sun is bright,
the view is stunning,

take flight!

Why linger
at the edge
of success?

Take courage,
spread your feathers,
test your muscle,

fledge!

Day 40

Pantsuit - Fall Guy - Yield

The *s* in the word pantsuit
does double duty,
as it is a pants suit.

The modern garment,
pants, is a single piece
of clothing, despite
having two legs,
so why the plural?

Perhaps because pantaloons
were two separate pieces,
one for each leg, like chaps.

Women were not allowed
to wear pants for centuries,
not even on horseback.

I was not allowed to wear
them in Catholic grade school.

What will it take to be
empowered as a woman?

Surely, it has to be more
that wearing a pantsuit.

The pantsuit did take women
in business and politics
out of their traditional skirts,

but not out of reach
of a rude legacy,
the demeaning
slang term, *skirt.*

At sixty-three,
I'm no longer willing to be
the fall guy, to be duped
or dumped on as scapegoat.

Why then do I still yield so easily
to stoic patriarchal itineraries,
most painfully those inscribed within me
as culturally appropriate roles
and long-standing female identities?

What will it mean
to step into a gender-free,
unbiased reality?

Helen Ready sang,
"I am woman, hear me roar
in numbers too big to ignore!"

Aren't women still not being heard?

I've held far too many
underpaid, underappreciated jobs
despite two academic degrees
that should have liberated me.

Eventually, I built my own business
as a voice coach, and that was rewarding.

I was able to empower young voices,
which ultimately can lead to the possibility
that these young people, especially women,
will have a clear voice in their own lives,
and will project that voice in larger society.

Now that I am retired,
I can be whatever I want to be
more deliberately. Writer, dancer,
comedian, community enhancer.

Even so, I feel I am not stepping
into my own full empowerment,
my truest, treasured identity.

How can I learn to yield
to my highest potentiality?

*Posing with a neighbor's classic car
in front of my opa and oma's house, age 5*

Day 41

Porgué - Flotar - Deleble
Why - Float - Erasable

"My Abuela says, some things happen
so that other things can happen."

from the film: "A Boy Called Sailboat"

¿Porgué?

Why did this take place?
No ideal reason appears.

Is it preliminary
to a crucial occurrence
of yet unknown import?

Flotar.

I float through my life,
like a tiny twig
in a wide river,

occasionally
finding an eddy,
or rushing through

narrow channels
of churning white water,

then drifting
on the reflective
surface of a placid lake.

Deleble.

Can I erase past pain
by tracing its pathways,
seeking out its origin
like a Dr. Livingston,
I presume, tracking denial
to its inevitable headwaters?

What is the source
of my malleable malaise?

Porgue.

Because other things
need to happen.

The complex chain
of linked events
in my lifetime,
is like a DNA strand,
or molecules aligning

to form peptides,
proteins, a cascade
of probabilities,

like a waterfall
forcefully depositing
the small twig
of my biography
downstream,

always downstream.

Day 42

Promissory - Repose - Discipline

Each morning,
a promissory note.

To rise from repose,
not knowing what awaits,

allowing hope to fill,
like camellia tea,
the cup of the empty day.

Happiness is a discipline,

a practice of attention
to the subtle details of joy.

Day 43

Confortable - Llaneza - Relucir
Comfortable - Simplicity - Shine, Stand out

I don't want to stand out
in a crowd, have no desire
to be noticed, or loud,

yet everything I do
is designed for vibrancy.

It's not about me,
it's about luminosity.

I am not comfortable
in the lime light,
will likely seek simplicity
over glitz and notoriety.

Yet, I wear bold clothes,
am not afraid to be the fool,
dance when others sit it out,
sing a capella jazz whenever
an opportunity calls,
have been told I am exotic
for wearing a hot pink
cowgirl hat and Peter Max
leggings to line dance class.

Obviously, I am hiding
in plain sight.

Can I learn to be at ease
with being unintentionally
a flamboyant cat?

Halloween, in a Goldie Hawn moment

Day 44

Venero - Bizmo - Impacto
Water spring - Poultice - Impact

This vereno,
high in these montañas,
flows up from the warm
womb of Mother Earth.

This sweet water rises,
gently calling
the butterfly maidens,
to dance over
the mossy banks.

Their moccasined feet,
a tender sweetgrass bizmo
for this depleted soil.

Their quiet songs
bring renewal,
a blossomed breath
of spiritual spring.

Every drop of this
agua sagrada
is curative.

Every kiss,

cada beso,
of dancing feet
on the tender skin
de La Madre Tierra.

is an honorable impact,
un impacto honorable,

es curativo.

Day 45

Mito - Sabor - Fineza
Myth - Flavor - Finesse

Mito

There is a myth I carry
as the core story
of my intimate identity.

Mostly, I am unaware
that this mito sways
my daily perceptions,
carves out the monuments
of what I believe to be so.

We all hold a story,
perhaps too closely,
of our *Once Upon a Time*,
inscribed by early experience,
now both eroded
by the slow pulsing river
of living, and hidden
by the sandy deposits
of embellished recalling.

Myth is socially ingrained
allegory, meant to make sense

of pathos and eros
through outsized archetypes.

It is a book we've all written
filled with our fondness
for fairytales, our need
to blindly bite into
the shiny, red apple
and sleep.

Sabor

Can I awaken
to taste, to savor

the actual flavors
of daily living,
free from craving escape,

released from grim fantasies,
and magical somedays?

Finezo

Imagine walking a tightrope,
arms outstretched,
welcoming the air,
mind focused so feet

can find the right tension
against the taut fibers.

I embrace the finesse
of keeping my eyes open
to each delicate step,
each precise movement
on this sky-high
balancing beam
of graciousness,

whether or not
there is
a safety net.

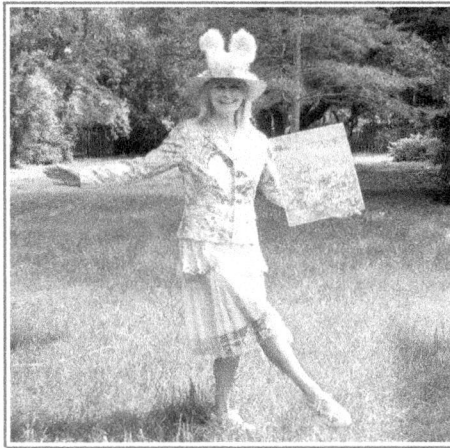

Easter dance

Day 46

Cercado - Translación - Esperanza
Enclosed - Translation - Hope

Cercado

To be enclosed in our own skin,
a world separate from all others,
yet so permeable, our human derma,
a loosely bound barrier, thin and fragile.

Translación

Moisture, medicine, emotion, all
translate across our soft membranes,
aid us to comprehend the language
of living: heat, cold, dull, sharp.

Esperanza

From within our enclosures, we reach out
to the haloes of translucence that sing
like choirs of light, knowing hope resides
just outside the veils we hide behind.

Day 47

Preludio - Elástico - Caritativo
Prelude - Elasticity - Charitable

Preludio

Is this life but a prelude,
the brief opening stanzas
of an epic poem beyond form?

Elástico

The body is flexible
to a degree, its endurance
relies on sustaining elasticity.

The mind and spirit
have greater resiliency.

So many practices
designed with strength
and flexibility in mind.

Yoga, meditation, Tai Chi,
mindful walking,
inspirational reading,
and listening to life,
always listening deeply.

They say practice makes perfect,
but what can be perfect?

Practice makes us malleable
in body, mind and spirit.

Caritativo

To be charitable to oneself is hard.
Far easier to give to others, to causes.

Charity is an act of compassion
based on the recognition that we
are not separate from other beings.

Keeping the heart strings elastic
is essential, knowing when to close,
when to open, and just how far.

Preludio

The prelude is an exquisite introduction.
Just listen deeply to the musical pieces
of J. S. Bach, of Frédéric Chopin.
Soak your senses in Claude Debussy's
Prélude à L'aprés-midi d'un Faune.

We are all such tender introductions
to the larger music beyond form.

Day 48

Capricho - Influgo - Remedio
Whim - Influence - Remedy

Capricho

Yesterday, the wind
went on an extended bender.

A derecho with gale force gusts
up to 100 mph, slapped against
everything like an angry, old drunk.

Whacking tree branches, buffeting
fiercely against the house, hissing
even through closed windows.

It sent the resin lawn chairs sailing
across the backyard like soccer balls
to an unknown goal, in its unleashed
capricho of epic proportions.

On the roof, the metal grates
of the evaporative cooler
squealed like mad banshees.

All afternoon, the derecho raged,
kicking up loose desert dust

until a low brown fog obscured
the mountains that loom closely
over this Tularosa Basin town.

A single robin sequestered
under a quivering oleander,
occasionally spreading her wings
to test the air, then quickly
retracting her flight feathers,
scurrying further back
under the protective foliage.

Influgo

Everything felt
the disturbing influence
of the turbulent,
incessant wind.

I was safely tucked away
inside the sturdy structure
of my own nesting place.

Watching the massive limbs
of an Afghan pine flail
as I gazed through the window,

I sat sewing curtains
to distract myself
from my animal nervousness,

yet, the turmoil
entered my soul.

Remedio

We were all waiting
for the remedy of sunset,

when the extreme
temperature differential
would cease,

and eventually
the dust would settle,

so that we could gaze up
and see the mountain peaks,

the reassurance of landmarks,
and of twinkling stars.

Day 49

Typewriter - Sway - Dust

My step-father, Johannes,
was a Dutch-born piano tuner.

He worked by ear and kept
a small shop where he refurbished
Steinways, Yahamas, Baldwins
and numerous pianos
of lesser-known brands,
both uprights, and lavish grands.

The shop was three blocks
from my elementary school,
Saint Emydius, the Patron Saint
of Earthquakes, situated as it was
in the foggy Ingleside district
of earthquake-prone San Francisco.

In the dark back office of the shop,
sat an old Underwood typewriter,
the heavy kind with the staunch
white keys stamped with black letters,
the metal strike bars, and an ink ribbon.

Johannes typed with his index fingers,
un-rhythmically, tic, tic-tic-tic, tic-tic,
invoices and occasional correspondence.

I coveted that clumsy Underwood,
a romantic icon of the writer's life,
which I aspired to live, even as a child.

Sadly, that old, funky typewriter
never made its way to me.

I did my BA in Creative Writing
on an electric Olivetti, then spent
years as a secretary on various
IBM Selectrics, typing endless letters
of no import to me, to make money.

Now, my wireless keyboard and iMac
make writing and editing a breeze
by comparison, and I doubt
I would dust off an Underwood
to go back to such outdated technology.

I rise and write early, and the violent
ticking of an antiquated machine
might wake up the household
and likely irritate the heck out of me.

I'll admit, romance has its sway.
I have gone online to find
antique Underwoods on eBay.

They are collectors items now,
requiring a hefty outlay
of up to a thousand dollars.

As I don't have the space
to display one as industrial art,
and the price is so surprisingly high,

I will leave the iconic machine,
dust-free, in my long-term memory.

Day 50

Notebook - Regenerate - Fortify

This little notebook
with its flexible pink cover
and its college-ruled pages
calling for composition,

is my morning companion,
my reliable confidant,
my meditative walk
through thought
and wandering emotion.

In its pages, I scribble
to clarify my randomized mind,
to discover what insight I might
glean from a regenerative night
of slumber and dreaming.

The writing is integral
to my preparation
for the dawning day.

Here, I fortify
my intentions, then
let myself enter
the flow of doing.

That momentum
will carry me through
to the evening.

Soon, this little notebook
will be filled to the last page,

and I will enjoy finding
its replacement,

so I can start anew.

In the cycle of my
private writer's life,

this familiar touchstone
centers all that I do.

Day 51

Logic - Scaffold - Enable

The New Mexico Museum
of Space History, here
in Alamogordo, hosts
an exhibit dedicated
to all things Star Trek.

There are cases filled
with various paraphernalia:
books authored by the actors,
dolls inspired by the characters,
recorded video interviews
looping in a viewing room,
and the bit worse for wear
original set of the transporter.

"Beam me up, Scotty!"

Did you know that this
most quoted phrase
was never actually spoken
in the 1966-69 TV series?

Included in the collection
are two first-edition books
by Leonard Nimoy.

I Am Not Spock,
published in 1976,
and *I Am Spock,*
published in 2015.

Make up your mind, Leonard.

Actually, I find
these humorously apposed
titles telling of Nimoy's
ultimately making peace
with being forever associated
with his iconic character,
who was all logic in order
to repress his intense
Vulcan emotions.

Logic is a scaffold,
a structure built to enable
the mind's nimble curiosity
and need for perpetual progress.

How sturdy it appears!
How willingly it forgets
its place as support,
usurping a grander purpose.

Pointed ears or not,
logic has its faults.

It can be two-dimensional,
leaving out depth perception,
which is a gift of emotional
intelligence, not reason.

What Spock would term
illogical, can be
another form of logos,
a knowing beyond
the mere concrete.

Einstein implied
logic should secede
to a higher calling,
claiming, "imagination
is more important
than knowledge."

In any case,
as Spock would say,
"Live long and prosper."

And, let me add,
give equal inclination
to the heart and remember
to always "Engage!"

Book cover, 1976 publication

Book cover, 2015 publication

Day 52

Comeback - Pretty - Tap

I'm the queen of the comeback.
Might have missed my calling
as a stand-up act, as I find humor
in pretty much anything.

I wore a jester's cap on the gurney
to x-ray after a major surgery.
Just trying to bring some levity
to a sterile, not-so-pretty scene.

I opt for laughter
to pull though pain,
or inevitable awkwardness.

A survival strategy, true, but
also a talent I'd like to tap into
with greater intentionality.

I was never the class clown,
though others might disagree.
I did read the daily announcements
in high school over the intercom
with my buddy, Marc Lalli.
We were a crack-up
morning improv routine.

I'd like to make a comeback.

My heavy-handed intellect needs
a regular infusion of helpless giggles.

I wrap my zinger philosophy
in Silly Putty, because I know
I take myself too seriously.

I'll understand completely,
if you don't understand me,

but it will be so much more fun
if you decide to really get me!

Day 53

Extravagant - Fabric - Phoenix

I once made a banner
out of felt and burlap
of a rising Phoenix bird
to hang as decoration
at my first wedding,
of all things!

With blue wings outstretched,
and a majestic plume
of emerald tail feathers,
she is crowned with red flames
in triumphant resurrection.

My mother saved the banner
for over thirty years,
and brought it back to me
all the way from the Netherlands,
when she visited Silver City.

The fabric, stained with decades
of patient aging, is sadly faded.

The extravagant colors too
are muted, perhaps worn out
from all that transmutation.
The brutal expression of renewal

the Phoenix represents
no longer appeals to me.

The gently folded mythic bird
rests in a chest in the garage,
hopefully safe from further
fiery transfigurations.

Rising from the ashes
seems needlessly dramatic,
even though I suppose
I still do it, upon occasion.

I'd like a new mascot,
one that doesn't require
recurrent cremation!

How about a hummingbird?

I painted a watercolor of one
years ago and she hangs,
perpetually cheerful,
near my bed, where she greets
me with her quiet beauty.

I choose her rainbow wings
and iridescent azure head.

No more harsh flames!
I want nectar instead!

Day 54

Forestry - Receive - Cast

The art of planting and caring
for a forest, is the mission of forestry.

The Mescalero Apache
are masters of this noble task.
They do not leave all dead wood
standing, only some for habitat.

The rest they clear using their horses,
debris being carefully gathered
in managed piles, and repurposed.

This gives the lofty ponderosa room
to breathe and sway, free from threat
of too easily ignited dry tinder.

In the Mescalero Apache forests
you can see the open sky and
watch golden eagles fly.

Ground cover too is managed,
not overgrown, or invasive.

We in the west fell living trees
without first asking to receive
their ancient blessings.

We cast aside the ideal
of the honorable harvest.
We sell off wild land
for timber and development.

Our Forest Service sets fires
on especially windy days in spring,
and calls them, *controlled burns.*
In these past few years, many
have gone woefully out of control.

Why not remove the dead timber,
much of which is bark beetle infested
and create pellets for fuel, rather
than leaving fuel for disaster?

Fires in the forest are natural,
a needed ritual of the sacred cycles,
but we create unnaturally dense
vegetation, and the resulting fires
are no longer regenerative,
they are devastatingly destructive,
taking everything.

We have a lot to learn
from the Mescalero Apache,
why not allow them to teach us?

Why not invite them as leaders
to be part of our forestry team?

Day 55

Unite - Essay - Regardless

How to unite the myriad
facets of our selves?

How to connect our hearts,
minds, doings, beings, all we bring
to our daily meanderings,
into a harmonious pattern
reflecting our values, quirks,
uniquely exquisite beauty?

Every day is an essay,
in both meanings of the word:
to attempt, to try; and
a composition from a personal,
therefore finite, point of view.

Regardless of our differences,
we are more united than divided
by countless commonalities of need,
and by our irrepressible desire
to express our hard-earned realities.

These miniature treatises of mine,
these tiny poetic essays, are my
attempts to try to make sense

for myself, and thus perhaps
by chance a tad for you,
of what we are doing here and why.

Today, let's essay for joy,
let's collect our spontaneous
miracles together, whether
in hand-woven sweetgrass baskets
or digital files on flickering screens,

let's try for generous actions
that generate pay-it-forward bliss,
creating a cascading fountain
of beneficent well-being.

Day 56

Tactile - Fringe - Benefactor

For over three decades,
I resided fifteen miles
from California's capitol,
Sacramento, *River City,*
and its splayed metropolis.

I now live at the base
of the Sacramento Mountains,
an odd coincidence of names,
only fifteen miles away
from what in winter
more resembles Alaskan wilderness
than southeastern New Mexico.

Up there, above 9000 feet,
grow Sitka spruce, ponderosa pine,
Douglas fir, aspen and hemlock.

The peak of Sierra Blanca,
with a head of pure white snow,
at 12,000 feet, gleams in the distance.

With a wind chill factor,
the cold is painfully tactile,
an icy embrace that lingers,

sends chills down your spine
and leaves your fingers aching.

That serious alpine climate
gives fringe benefits
to those living far below.

In the heart of winter,
these formidable mountains
protect the lower core
of the Tularosa Basin
from the severe storms
wreaking havoc on Texas
and Oklahoma to the east.

On summer nights,
they provide cooling downdrafts
with occasional blessed rains.

It's a nice arrangement.

Day 57

Telepathy - Level - Compass

Last night, I dreamt
of my deceased
ex-husband, Gregory.

He was late. I was waiting.
The dream was the waiting.

Are dreams a type of telepathy?
More than mere processing
of the day's random mysteries?

I desire better tools
with which to decipher life.

A carpenter's steady level
with an air bubble,
letting me know
when things are sloped.

A compact compass,
small enough to carry
always in the palm
of my heart, so that I can be
certain I am facing true north,
not heading south,
as the saying goes.

If dreams are messages,
why did Gregory appear,
at the edge of my consciousness?

What is his gift of insight?

He was an expert carpenter,
a wood whisperer
with an art degree,
a fastidious astronomer,
and avid outdoorsman.

Is he trying to offer me
his level and compass?

If so, Gregory,
I accept.

Day 58

Assemblage - Organize - Invocation

Assemblage is art
brought together
from bits and pieces,
random odds and ends,
the contents of a hundred
junk drawers, the flotsam
and jetsam of the ordinary.

The trick in the process
is how to organize
this cultural debris
into a sculptural fantasy.

Using a hot glue gun
and the creative adhesive
of an evolving theme,
humor and irreverence
lead to odd juxtapositions
as vehicles of meaning.

My personal assemblage,
Surf's Up, Duck!
with its word play title conjuring
Bugs Bunny's famous quip,
is an homage to the subculture
of surfing, a whimsical tribute

to the aquatic daydreams
of a land-locked, desert dweller.

It's a comical contrivance,
but beneath the frivolity lies
my genuine invocation
to all things ocean,
an exposure of my dolphin
spirit's longing for home.

Art as quirky self-portraiture.

Surf's Up, Duck! Assemblage by Eve

Day 59

Rosewater - Illegible - Discombobulate

Rosewater, so associated
with religious pilgrimage,
soul journeys, the inward
casting of the heart's glance.

A translucent liquid
with a mere hint of scent,
an innocent, unassuming
perfume, reminiscent
of pre-pubescence.

Not a passionate presence,
almost never distilled from red,
only pink and yellow petals.

An old-fashioned concoction,
from a grandmother's half-empty
long-necked, crystal bottle
residing placidly on a dark-wood
dresser in late-day sunlight.

A roseate perspective
on a now illegible life.

Surely, there was strife,
worry, loss, all the usual human
heartaches, plenty to ponder,
enough to discombobulate,

but what lingers
is this remainder
of sweetness mixed
with an edge of regret
that faded roses
almost always beget.

Day 60

Cameo - Clue - Crave

On a rain-slicked evening
in the city of San Francisco,
I lost a precious memento,
a cameo photo of my oma.

My maternal grandmother's
smiling face was embraced
by the silver case of a pinned
broach I wore on my sweater,
well-hidden below a raincoat,
nonetheless, it broke free.

Why I was wearing it at all
in such inclement weather
is a mystery to me, but losing it
caused all manner of sorrow.

All along the steep sidewalk
of Noe Street, where the gutters
had turned to rivulets,
I searched for her features,
so much like my own,
round shape, slender nose,
thin lips, high cheek bones.

I crave any vestige of my heritage,
being an immigrant kid.

Mementos like that photo,
not quite the size of a quarter,
ought to have stayed safely
in a jewelry box or drawer.

I wore her against my heart
for comfort and because
I feel precious things
stored away in the dark
are hardly there at all.

I prefer to visit with them
on a regular basis, even
at the cost of their
potential harm
or disappearance.

The weak streetlights
made wavering haloes
on the wet pavement.

Even had I seen a glint
of the silver case,
that delicate photo
would likely already
have succumbed

to the dampness,
her face erased.

My two housemates
helped me scour
the path we'd walked
from our pseudo-Victorian
to whatever venue
had called us out.

It was 1980, I believe.
We were all in college then.

That was over 40 years ago,
yet just the word cameo
brought my oma's tiny photo
instantly back to mind.

It occurs to me now,
for the first time maybe,
that I could find another
photo of my oma, Johanna,
make a copy and place
her face into a locket.

I can replace what was lost
on that long ago blustery evening
with a new keepsake to hold closely
for the joy of reminiscing.

Day 61

Keynote - Reunion - Crackerjack

My advice to myself.

Go ahead and accept
the honor of being
the keynote speaker
at your own reunion,
the bringing together
of all those disparate
selves you carry.

After all, weren't you voted,
Most likely to succeed,
by your classmates
as a high school senior?

At a reunion luncheon,
that *most likely* listings page
of the school paper was displayed.

Someone asked,
"So, did you?"

It stumped you.
"Did I what?"

"Succeed?" he queried.

Certainly not in the ways
most people gauge success,
you thought, but didn't say.

Instead, you said
something like,
"If staying true
to your own creative soul,
no matter what,
is success, then yes."

The man with the query
looked at you as if
you'd just spoken in Greek.

Then he smiled,
"That makes sense,"
he said, "I guess."

So here's my keynote speech.
I'll keep it short and sweet.

Just do a crackerjack job
of being your dearest self.

Figuring out what that might mean
is the heart of the journey.

The world will want you
to conform, to follow

all kinds of norms
and make no waves.
But be brave enough
to stand out in a crowd.

Being loud is not your cup
of tea, so do it quietly.

Leave the cookie cutter
in the kitchen drawer.
You are meant to be more
than a carbon copy
of any latest trend.

Befriend yourself
enough to be authentic.

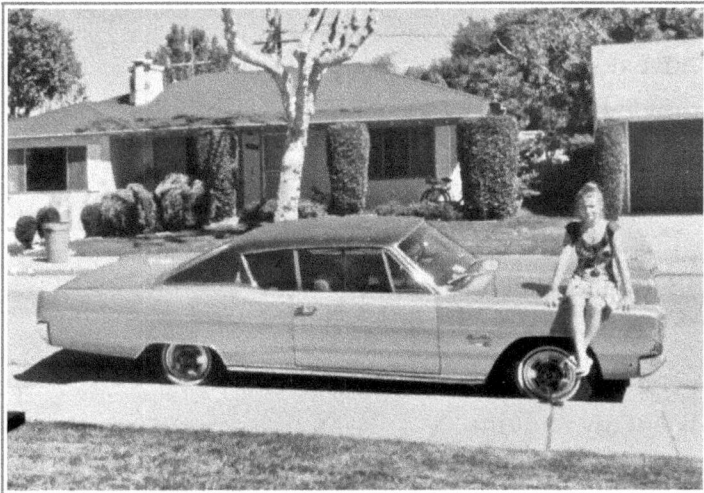

In high school with my first car

Day 62

Prescience - Identify - Tensile

Before I was born,
my mother did not know,
with scientific certainty,
if I was a girl or a boy.

She felt my energy
had tons of yang chi,
though she would not
have used that terminology.

Her prescience, not to mention
all of my fervent kicking, convinced
her I was a soccer-playing boy.

I have a recording
of my own birth cry,
transferred from reel-to-reel,
and my mother's tearful,
joyous voice repeating,
with obvious surprise at my gender,
Een meisje! Een meisje!

My energy remains
quite masculine,
my mind being trained
by a male academy.

Despite the many and varied
agonies that being female
has visited upon me,
and having lost along the way
some of the internal anatomy
that identifies a body as such,
my sense of self is oddly
gender neutral.

I haven't seen a box
to check for that, as yet.

I wrote a blues song once
titled, *My Soul is Neither
Man Nor Woman.*

My birth name, Brigitte,
is the French version
of the Irish name *Brighid,*
Old Irish, *Brigit,*
from old Celtic *Brigantī.*

In Irish mythology,
it's the name of the goddess
of fire, poetry and wisdom.

Well, I'd like to say that suits me!

Brigitte is still my legal middle name.

I was named after a character
on a radio show with a voice
so melodious and tender
my mom fell in love with it,
and named me Brigitte.

When I arrived in America
at age seven, no one was able
or willing to pronounce it correctly.

At Catholic grade school, the nuns
instantly called me Bridget, the Irish
name being a natural fit there.
That pronunciation continued
all through high school and college.

Just before graduate school,
when I'd moved to an entirely
new location, I changed
my name to Eve. It was an act
of defiance against the shame
foisted upon Adam's partner
by a misogynistic church.

Eve is the Hindu goddess
who named all things
in the original garden.

As a poet, I too am one who names.

As I see it, the symbolic eating
of the apple in Eden, which proffered
the knowledge of good and evil,
is a powerful act of evolution.

Yet, the name Eve still carries
the stain of misinterpretation,
no matter what I may think or say.

I've thought of making
another name change,
but it's a major bureaucratic hassle,
and change it to what, pray tell?

There is great tensile strength
in carrying your own true name.

None of my three names,
Eve, West or Bessier
are my own by birth.

I also chose the name Eve
because it's a lovely palindrome.
West comes to me from a dear mentor.
Bessier from a French great-grandmother.

Brigitte Desiree Boerebach,
my actual birth name,
provides endless probabilities
for mispronunciation.

I also have no desire, although
Desiree was my middle name,
to carry on the patriarchy
of a father who abandoned me at three.

I guess, I'm still a character
on this long-running radio show
in search of my own moniker.
One that will best express
my gender-neutral though
mentally masculine self-identity.

I've toyed with being
simply Eve West.

My maternal grandparents
were Johannes and Johanna.

I've thought of using Jo West
in their honor. But in Spanish,
so prevalent in the southwest,
the J is pronounced like an H.
The result would be, Ho West.
Not exactly what I'm going for!

Perhaps, going back to Brigitte
is the answer after all.
Albeit folks always say it
immediately back to me as,
"Nice to meet you, Bridget!"

Day 63

Bud - Pluck - Sustain

The ornamental cherry,
blooming like a sea
of opened pink umbrellas
floating up, quivering
into a sky of puffy white.

Each ornate flower bud
wearing Geisha lipstick,
waiting for bee kisses
to pluck its ochre pollen
and transport potent,
sticky beads from stamen
to stigma, to ovule.

To sustain its own life,
the tree originates a tsunami
of beauty. Breathe deeply
the sweet aroma of perpetual
conception before the blooms
fade and maroon leaves
replace tender hopeful petals.

Day 64

Confidence - Relate - Laid-back

To relax, fully relax
with confidence
in one's well-being,
is a foreign feeling
I'd like to learn to relate to
on a daily basis.

I normally don't possess
a laid-back kind of mind.

Slacking off at all
has never been my luxury,
but I'm willing to buy into
a more hammock-style life.

Swaying lazily
to and fro, in the embrace
of a cradle made of rope
is a perfect recipe for mellow.

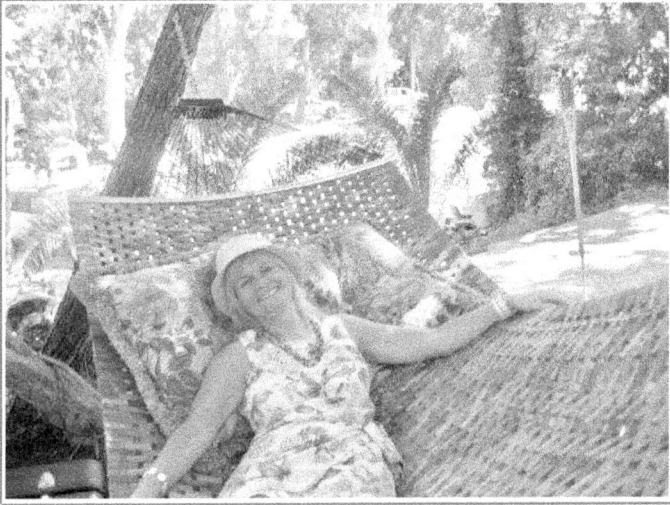

A mellow moment in a friend's hammock

Day 65

Technical - Certitude - Inception

Technicians of the Sacred,
is an impressive collection
of poetry and incantations
gathered by Jerome Rothenberg
from global indigenous cultures.

To think of the sacred
as requiring technique
is a unique perspective.

Modern cultures do certify
religious leaders, require
they complete specific trainings,

but how do we devise
with certitude what a leader
needs to know about the growth
of the soul, and how to teach
the techniques to reach it?

How do we authorize
any one person to supervise
and lead others in the pursuit
of attaining enlightenment?

Shaman are trained
from a very young age.
Successive Dalai Lama
are searched out painstakingly
as they are believed
to be reincarnated Buddhist
leaders at inception.

We expect technical expertise
from career specialists:
dentists, doctors, plumbers,
mechanics, architects.

Do we not need to insist upon
an even higher level of competence
from those to whom we entrust
the guidance of our spiritual lives?

Day 66

Rainmaker - Freelance - Evoke

Rainmaker is a Hopi kachina
of awesome meteorological power.

A carved cottonwood doll
by G. Pooley, a tummy-hugger
version of this revered figure,
stands in my bookcase, facing east.

These small kachinas
were popular keepsakes
in the hay-day of Route 66
travel through northern Arizona.

When rain is in short supply
I take him out under the sky.

Today might be an apt occasion
for his ancient weather dance.

While an overabundance
of moisture is creating havoc
all around us, our ground is dry.

Rainmaker is a freelance dancer
traveling where the need is greatest.

He shakes his gourd rattle,
raises his low voice
to evoke potential storms,
even on a perfectly blue,
apparently cloudless day.

I've heard thunder reply
to his incantations,
felt icy rain on my face
when his song was sung.

I wonder if Rainmaker
is also the one to call
when atmospheric rivers,
one after another,
keep pummeling
the already soaked
and flooded land.

Is there a song and dance
that will stop relentless rain
from falling when the earth
is plentifully replenished
and calls for no more downpours?

Day 67

Oodles - Highlight - Crossroad

On days this winter
of sun and little wind,
opportunities occurred
for oodles of fun playing
Gong Pong in the park.

Gong Pong is liberted
ping pong with a twist.

Next to the kid's play area,
with its vibrant blue tarp,
sits and elegant ping pong table
made of concrete and granite.
The net is metal, and that's
where the oodles come in.

In regulation ping pong,
the woven net is taut,
and stops the ball.

In no-rules Gong Pong,
the net is solid metal
and returns the ball
back to the player
with a delicate gong,

reminiscent of a Buddhist temple.
Hence the name of the game.

The ball may remain in play,
for a succession of gongs.
Double-gongers, great wordplay.
Tripple-gongers, Quadruple-gongers.
Gong! Gong! Gong! Gong!

Keeping the ball on the table
is the goal, no points involved.
Balls may also rick-i-shay off
the top of the black metal net
ascending in any direction.

Uproarious laughter
is a regular highlight
of this kooky new game.

Right before the pandemic
rocked our daily realities,
I bought a professional
ping pong table from Joola.

We played in our garage
to MoTown and the Beatles
all through our sequestering.
It helped keep us sane.

Last year, when everything

we owned went into storage
with the future unknown,
the table had to be sold.
There just wasn't room for it.

That was a heartbreak for me.

Playing Gong Pong here in the park
is a crossroad from this past year
of extended stress, worry and pain,
into having a happy childhood again.

Gong! Gong! Gong! Gong!
Live long and Gong Pong!

The Gong Pong Table

Live long and Gong Pong!

Day 68

Mantra - Stroll - Camera

Evergreens are my morning mantra.
Seeing their needled sheen in sunlight
against a backdrop of high-altitude,
almost indigo blue, puts my mind at ease.

In these past three days, we've planted
eleven Emerald Green Arborvitae,
Thuja occidentalis, of the cypress family.

These sturdy little evergreens will eventually
shield us from forceful seasonal winds.

We're placing our faith in these baby trees.
Someday, their stout conical shapes will be
our vibrant privacy screen, and we'll be
surrounded by their plush green.

The trees will take years to reach
the height we'll want them to be,
so they are an investment in seeding
a home here on this 0.16 acre property
in a vast valley, under imposing mountains
providing a watershed to this dry lakebed,
which holds human footprints formed 22,000
years ago, and as many ancient petroglyphs.

Soon, I will stroll again amongst those
carved drawings on black volcanic rock,
depicting figures and symbols of ancient
cultures who lived here in the Tularosa Basin
beneath stunning views of the snow-capped
Sacramento Mountains hovering above.

Such an immense, open landscape
can become a mantra under foot.

Its outsized scale escapes
accurate capture on camera.

While I still prefer a forest of ponderosa,
which is blessedly not far away,
in my day to day, this outrageously
vast terrain is starting to grow on me,
with its Lady of the Mountain escarpment,
distant Oscura peak silhouettes, and glittering
gypsum gleaming from a distance like the lake
that once filled this basin with reeds and fishes.

This out-of-the-way place, this vast terrain,
will teach me its unique spiritual rituals,
its own wry language of the still untamed,
equestrian desperado, wild western spirit.

Day 69

Transcend - Imbue - Beatific

Language is a sixth sense.

Senses are a gift of being able
to interpret the physical,
to make our way through
the maze of experience
by using sight, smell, hearing,
taste and tactile sensation.

Language lets us make sense
of our physical dimensions,
but also transcends form,
allowing us to be intimately
involved with the immensely
beatific nature of reality.

Language provides signposts
for emotional navigation.
A compass of words,
accurately gauged, provides
clear direction for the expression
of hard to define feelings.

Without language, the pure
visceral experience of living
still exists, but there is no way

to precisely convey the sensations.

Birds have songs, as do frogs,
and whales and other creatures.
Even trees send messages between
their root systems and through air
by their chemical excretions.

All life forms use codes of meaning
but only we use words, and so many!
Tens of thousands for each language,
and there are 7,139 officially known
languages on our small blue planet.

Why then are we choosing
to lose this rich sixth sense
by using only consonants,
cryptic codes and emojis
easily texted with two thumbs?

Our amazing opposable thumbs
are designed for better things,
like holding and sharing
in the real world,
not just in cyberspace.

Are we not aware
that we will numb
one of our most
powerful senses

when we choose to lose
rich communication?

Why sacrifice such unique
potential for elation?

Words are vessels of magic
that imbue meaning.

They are a means to relate
to the wonders of the cosmos.

Day 70

Glassblowing - Catch - Tone

Who invented glass,
devised this unexpected
molecular revision?
I'm sure it was a progression
of steady discovery.

No one stands on a beach
of silica sand and says,
these gleaming single grains
that pour through my fingers
could become a translucent
substance from which
we can drink our wine,
and with which
we can keep the wind
from entering our houses,
without enclosing ourselves
in un-natural darkness.

Then again, maybe someone
did stand on a long strand
of white sand, sun in their eyes,
and thought exactly that.

It's extreme heat that does it,

transforms silica to glass.
Volcanoes have been at it
since the Eocene, making
hard, black, glossy obsidian,
which cavemen later carved
to tip their primitive spears.

It would be many millennia
of years before the Syrians
in the 1st Century adapted
the earliest glass workings
of the Mesopotamians
and Egyptians to bring
a new technique into existence.
The art of glassblowing
makes every day and luxury
vessels catch the light,
and hold us transfixed
by this chemical magic.

The physical strength
and endurance needed
to wield the molten silica
to and from a 2000 degree
Fahrenheit furnace, and turn
its burning weight like a glob
of sun at the end of the metal pipe
through which air is blown,
is nothing short of awesome and builds
the muscle tone of a Samson.

Miraculously,
it's human breath
that imbues molten glass
with its ornate shapes.

To view the glassblowing
genius of Dale Chihuly,
is to know that this intensely
laborious art in the proper
hands forges gorgeous forms.

Chihuly's candy-hued bowls
with their satin textures,
swirl like the rings of Saturn,
expand like the spiral
shape of our Milky Way Galaxy,
and glow like clam shells
holding hidden pearls
of artistic perfection.

Entranced by kaleidoscopic
glass, we are transported
to a luminous fairyland
of other-worldly wonder.

Day 71

Outpost - Merit - Grace

New Mexico is a state of distance,
an arrangement of outposts
from earlier centuries along historic
trade routes like the Santa Fe
and Butterfield Trails, and the
notorious Jornada del Muerto.

New Mexico's history
is a testament to diversity.

Ancient and contemporary
pueblo dwellers, Apache
and Comanche horsemen,
Navajo nomadic herders,
Conquistador explorers,
over-zealous clergymen,
hopeful pioneer families,
and a smattering of famous
gun slingers, all risked life
and limb to come into this blending
of high desert and impressive mountain
terrains, decked in snow and conifers.

All managed to stay and make
their daily way on these isolated mesas.

Their daring demands respect,
perhaps even the mettle
of those whose actions
were notoriously of dubious merit.

Despite desolate,
far-flung topographies
and desiccated arroyos,
Nuevo Mexico holds
its own brand of grace,

a buoyancy of pure light,

a furious firing of the imagination
that overwhelming vastness elicits,

a unique perspective on the divine
that four horizons stretching
into copious emptiness inspires.

Day 72

Grouchy - Instill - Upbeat

I woke up grouchy.
When the day is barely
on its feet, how can there be
any reason for crankiness?

It's yesterday's snafus, lingering
with a bitter aftertaste,
that need addressing
and leave me peeved.

It has to do with taxes,
and health insurance,
the usual human drudgeries
overseen by bureaucracies,
those behemoth slow-moving
beasts of proletariat burden.

For me, the trick will be
to instill confidence
in a day that's already
had most of the air
let out of it from the get go.

How do I retrieve an upbeat
state of mind, while bravely

facing the unavoidable hassles
that lie ahead of me?

It's odd how easily a mood
can get away from you,
apparently out of your control,
raging with its own teenaged,
stubborn craving for pathos.

A lasso is the appropriate tool,
to corral the wild horses
of discontent, that whinny
and buck, refusing their saddles.

I completely get their resistance,
would gladly set them free,
but adult responsibilities
are weighing down on me,
and I have no other opportunity
but to heed the call of duty.

How did we end up here?
I can't imagine we all agreed
to be so heavily domesticated.

Yesterday, I visited the local zoo
to bring some child-like levity.

The baby animals bouncing about
or suspended in their hammocks

were cute, undeniably, yet viewed
through their metal cages,
their playful behaviors
teased out a taste of irony.

Yet, I won't get all mushy
by declaring that these animals
should be set free. Let me
instead observe their luxury.

In a well-maintained zoo,
the animals enjoy daily food
of good nutrition, freedom
from constant vigilance
and the fear of perdition.

When illness or injury strike,
they have veterinarians
at the ready. No wild animal
has this kind of carefree life.

The parallels do not escape me.

Taxes and bureaucracies
provide us with needed services.

Unless we grow our own,
our food too is brought to us
by outside providers.

If we are lucky enough to live
in a well-maintained society,
our health too is monitored
and supported by professionals.

Our major predators are generally
locked away in their own cells,
and we are free to safely roam about
in our enclosures, play with our toys,
and laze in hammocks or sofas
when we are not working
to maintain the establishments
that keeps us fed and contented.

If we were now to agree
to set ourselves completely free
from all of the societal structures
and strictures we've self-imposed,
by what choices and agency
would we arrange it?

What would such freedom
actually mean in stark reality?

Vigilante justice? Food scarcity?
Early death by rotten teeth?

The natural pecking order
fueled by lower-brainstem behaviors

would quickly make sure
aggressive bullies got plenty,
while the rest of us cowered
in fear and went hungry.

So, is the answer simply
to live as freely as possible
within the current constricts
of our modern social contracts?

Don't look at me.
I don't have the answer.

Not today, in any case.

Remember, I woke up grouchy.

But in my cranky state,
I am happy to relay
these relevant questions.

Day 73

Haiku - Child - Rest

This morning's haiku,
a child's bad dream that lingered.
Birds sang it to rest.

Goldfinch, watercolor by Eve

Day 74

Falcon - Figure - Undaunted

A female peregrine falcon sits
on the edge of a narrow ledge,
just shy of the barbed-wired
under the high-rise roofline.

Her bright eyes scan
the urban canyon below,
which is filled with a slow-flowing
river of yellow taxi traffic,
near the green expanse
of New York's Central Park.

Undaunted in her hunt,
she alights. Using strong wings,
she quickly enters a thermal,
rises and circles high over the city.

Finding her target
down below, a lone pigeon,
she folds her wings and talons
into dive position, and plummets
earthward like a smart missile.

Capable of speeds
up to 200 miles per hour,

she can kill her prey
in mid-air upon impact,
even between structures of steel.

But the lowly pigeons
are fighter pilots too,
and can outmaneuver her.

She needs to eat soon,
pursues her prey with precision,
falling in controlled recklessness
towards the concrete street.

She and the pigeon careen,
making jagged sweeps,
in rollercoaster formations.

Mere moments before
pigeon, falcon and concrete
meet head on, the peregrine
corrects course one last time
and finds her prey gripped
tightly in her muscular talons.

Swooping upward in a daring,
last-resort arc, she heads back
to open sky to find a safe place
where she can finally dine.

Day 75

Recalcitrant - Glimmer - Enough

I desire to be more recalcitrant.
What is gained by being timid,
perpetually restrained?

In a recent dream,
all of the oppressive forces
that forged me, compressed me
more and more tightly until,
in a flash of light, every atom
of carbon in my body turned
into diamond resplendency.

I began to expand, and expand,
growing taller, larger, stronger.

I became a valiant, red-caped
superhero, capable of immense
physical strength and resilience.

I was recalcitrant, unrestrained.

I gained such prowess
as to be completely freed
from all past weakness,
released from all grievances.

When I awakened,
I was shaken,
felt my muscles ache
as though I'd truly been
flying through the sky,
red cape a banner behind me,
defeating mean villains,
rescuing all victims
of self-inflicted timidity.

Initially, I felt glad
to be small,
to be meek again.

But then the dream activated
something latent within me,
a glimmer of potential energy,
a hidden capacity needing
to be mined, not undermined.

Do I possess enough courage
to willfully embody it? Yes!

Day 76

Dogwood - Nerve-wracking - Ask

A year ago today,
we were in Virginia,
feeling frail
on the tail end
of a nerve-wracking,
month-long journey
to find a place to live.

My partner wanted
to move to Roanoke
to be close to his mom.

Every day for three weeks,
we'd driven down highways
lined with bare deciduous trees
hung with dry, creepy kudzu.

The forests so freaky
they reminded me
of that scene in Disney's
film, where Snow White
is lost in a winter woods,
bare trees reaching out
menacingly, frightfully.

The houses we found
online looked quite nice
in the expertly edited photos,
but always turned out
to be hideous, one was
actually falling into a sinkhole!

After exhausting miles
to go see them in person,
ending up as far
south as Tennessee,
trying unsuccessfully
to keep one step ahead
of real estate investors,
the houses were all dives.

During that arduous trip,
I'd asked the powers that be
to see at least one
blooming dogwood tree
before we needed to leave.

I'd heard that they are
a real southern treat,
and a treat was seriously needed!

In the final week,
every bare tree
planted in the vicinity
of the condo complex

where we were renting,
suddenly burst into bloom
with a profusion of pink
and white flowers.

I'd been surrounded
by dogwoods all along.

Ask and ye shall receive.

Day 77

Candor - Pianissimo - Flicker

When truth is loud,
it is easy to hear,

unavoidably close
to the outer ear.

Candor
can be boisterous.

More subtle
yet bold
spiritual reality

is spoken quietly,

like a pianissimo passage
of inner melody,

revealed in crystalline
moonlight, a mere flicker

of holistic insight.

Day 78

Minuet - Stringed - Biorhythm

Picture a minuet,
the slow, stately,
meticulous movements.

Partners in pairs,
weaving about the space,
hands barely touching,
bodies discretely placed.

The music, played
by stringed instruments,
may be occasionally festive,
but mostly stays gentile
in three-quarter meter.

A quaint parlor scene
from a BBC mini-series
of a Jane Austin tale.

A gaggle of young women
with flushed, fresh faces
in blush-colored lace dresses,
hoping to steal a glance
from a passing nobleman.

The dance as example
of the conservative
biorhythm of an age
of tightly regulated
social order and strata,
when a woman's chance
at advancement
was proffered solely
by a man's standing.

Better learn to minuet
perfectly, be alluring
but not flamboyantly pretty.

Day 79

Ukulele - Native - Dwell

The ukulele is not native
to the Hawaiian islands.

It traveled there with vaqueros,
cowboys from Mexico.

Hawaiian ranching precedes
the cowboy era of the American
west by three decades.

The Hawaiian cowboy,
the paniolo, is no Eastwood
He is sweet, sings to his horse
and wears a flower lei
on his vaquero sombrero.

His mellow-toned,
diminutive guitarro
has grown into the beloved
sound we all associate
with the Pineapple State.

While traditional Hula
is danced to spare rhythms
played on various gourds
and with resonant sticks,

more contemporary
Hawaiian music features
ukulele and slide guitar.

I sing in Hawaiian,
an endangered language.

I am not a native of
the Hawaiian islands,
but as part of a duo
called *Blonde Aloha*,
I honor the musical heritage.

While I am not able to dwell
on beloved Maui, as she's
quite a pricy paradise,
the Kodachrome island
remains my heart's home,

though I have not stepped foot
on her hibiscus-kissed shores
for over twenty-four years.

Day 80

Fluid - Ordinary - Bias

Heat can transmute
a solid to a fluid

give molecules
elbow room
through movement

Stone to magma
Ice to rivers and clouds

Ordinary thoughts
rattled around
by the heat of inspiration

lead to extraordinarily
brilliant explorations

that burst into actions
cut against the bias
of cultural convention

with the revolutionary
intention to change
the course of history
of her-story

We need a heating up
of collective imagination

a global consensus
of peaceful cohabitation

through the bubbling up
of higher aspirations

for our spiritually attainable
enlightened destination

Day 81

Scent - Pliant - Below

The blooming apple tree,
growing in the dark soil
below the far edge
of the wooden deck,
flavors the evening
with the scent
of gentleness.

In the quickening wind,
the adjacent
Himalayan cedar
is pliant, swaying.

The sturdy apple's
branches, thick and aged
remain immobile.

While her white,
laced with pink blossoms,
filled with industrious bees,
float ever so delicately
on the teasing breeze.

To stay steadfast
at the core,
yet receptive
through flexibility

as life proffers
the inevitable
unexpected,

is to be set free.

Day 82

Evident - Audition - Plateau

The purpose of life
is not precisely evident.

Why am I here?
A common enough question.

Why am I *here*, specifically
in this place, this time,
his particular existence?

An even deeper,
perplexing quandary.

Is life a type of audition,
a trying out for a larger role,
for a promotion to a more
advanced plateau?

Or is the meaning
found exclusively
in the immediate,
in the moment
we are experiencing?

I don't know,
but I believe the answer

lies in loving life
in each peculiar facet,
more and more,

inclusive of all suffering,
and of every joy,
in all of our confusion,
error and success.

I believe life is both
the audition
and the show.

How we handle
daily situations
creates the nature
of our next adventure
in understanding
a more holistic
consciousness,

always in service
of honoring
all that is.

Day 83

Vital - Mileage - Foresee

My 1997 Honda CR-V
has bravely accumulated
a healthy sum of mileage.

Her odometer currently
reads a hefty 185,290.
My mechanic insists
she's still a baby!

Well over 100,000
of those miles accrued
while I've been her driver.

The previous owner bought
her brand new, and told me
the small-town dealership
had a party with balloons
to welcome the arrival
of Honda's innovative model,
the Compact Recreational Vehicle.

It was the first of its kind,
along with the Toyota RAV-4,
to hit the American roadways.

Now the style proliferates.
A 4-wheel drive truck frame
with a comfortable sedan body
and lots of storage space
for your accoutrements.

The day I drove my Honda home,
I could not foresee the diversity
of the far and wide journeys
I would take in her sturdy,
boxy, emerald-green chassis.

We all accumulate mileage;
in our vehicles, in our experiences,
and in our hearts, so tightly packed
with every possible emotion.

The totals on our personal
odometers roll over and over
into the hundreds of thousands
as the decades rapidly pass.

It takes motion
to acquire mileage.

The odometer of a car
never driven will stick
at a static zero, even though
the vehicle's parts slowly

lose integrity, and become
worn with time.

A heart never tried
in the turmoil of love,
will age only in muscle.

It's intended destiny
is to be moved.

Motion is vital to life,
unavoidable, yet
too much of it
can be dizzying.

With all of the changes
I've been through
in these past two years,
we've all been through
in this era of pandemic
and political peril,

I'm happy my iconic car
is still traveling with me,
a trusted companion
on the road of my
ever-evolving life
topography.

Day 84

Handstand - Denim - Prayer

When I was a pre-teen,
I loved to do handstands
with my feet up against
the side of the house
for better balance.

I turned the world
upside down,
made the sky
into the ground,
covered with a patchwork
carpet of cumulus clouds.

The paisley triangles
of cotton cloth sewn
into the cut-open legs
of my denim jeans
to create bell bottoms,
went flying like prayer flags
suspended from my
sun-kissed ankles.

Day 85

Multiple-choice - Exchange - Bungalow

How do you answer
a multiple-choice question,
when all of the options
appear erroneous?

Offering multiple choices
makes the assumption
that no-one actually knows
the answer to the question
without first seeing it listed
among other, obviously
or not so obviously,
incorrect options.

Here's an example.

Question:
In the Beatles' song,
*The Continuing Story
of Bungalow Bill,*
what did Bill kill?

A. an elephant
B. his mother
C. a tiger
D. all of us

And then there is the lame,
annoying addition of:

E. none of the above

Which doesn't even attempt
to answer the question,

though in this case it does,
and answers it correctly, maybe.

Can I please exchange
my multiple choices
for an essay test?

I'd like to more fully express
my understanding.

My answer to the question
at hand would be this.

From the song lyrics,
we don't know what, if anything,
Bill actually killed.

However, the song implies
that giving a civilian
bungalow dweller
with some un-named rage

a gun, for hunting elephants,
or other things, might be
a point-blank bad idea.

Then again, who knows
what John and Paul intended.

As an intriguing segue,
here's the text of
the Second Amendment.

"A well regulated Militia,
being necessary to the security
of a free State, the right
of the people to keep
and bear Arms,
shall not be infringed."

Perplexing, yes?

Is that only the people currently
in the well-regulated Militia?
Or, is that every Bungalow Bill?

A dangerous ambiguity,
if you ask me.

Some say, let's exchange
guns for unbiased education,
a noble enough suggestion.

Is there such a thing
as unbiased education?

A. Yes
B. No
C. I don't understand the question
D. All of the above
E. None of the above

Day 86

Bohemian - Postulate - Fixture

Here are two definitions
of the bandied about,
somewhat coveted
term, Bohemian.

Both come from
the American Heritage
Dictionary of the English
Language, 5th Edition.

1. A person with artistic
or literary interests who
disregards conventional
standards of behavior.

2. A native or an inhabitant
of Bohemia, a crown land
and kingdom of the Austrian
empire.

The early Bohemians
of the first definition date back
to fifteenth-century France,
but we tend to think of the
subculture as founded

by the creative giants
of late 19th and early
20th century Paris,
specifically in Montmartre.

They were a collective
of mostly male writers,
painters and philosophers
disregarding conventional
standards of behavior.

They were daily fixtures
at Parisian sidewalk cafes,
consuming large quantities
of strong coffee and alcohol
while talking radical politics.

They painted naked showgirls,
wrote novels about bullfighting,
and poems about language.

Almost all of the famous
characters associated
with the term Bohemian,
in the first definition,
were in some manner
independently wealthy enough
to live in relative poverty
in order to focus solely

on their personal creativity.

While their ideals might
have been anti-bourgeoisie,
they themselves were
almost entirely from
working-class families.

I can safely postulate
that I am not Bohemian,
in either meaning of the word,

despite my love of writing,
music and visual art, and my
working-class upbringing,

I'm not so sure if I've ever
disregarded conventional
standards of behavior,
though you may beg to differ.

I have always struggled
to make a living outside
of my personal creative life,
making me rather too tethered
to be considered a free radical.

I did wear a Tyrolean dress
made for me by my mom
when I was six.

I suppose that's as close
as I've gotten to being
a real Bohemian,
but that's just style,
not substance.

I have upon occasion,
and much to my surprise,
been called a *Beat Poet*.

It's true that I do
write poetry to jazz,
and can embellish
my linguistic lines
with well-executed
vocal scat improvisations.

If that makes me a *Beat*,
then Shidoop-adap-dee, so be it!

In my Tyrolean dress, age six

Day 87

Double Take - Anapest - Recoup

*"Better **dwell** in the **midst** of alarms···"* William Cowper

Double take
is not technically an anapest,
a metrical foot of two unaccented
syllables followed by an accented one,

but just run through double,
then spice up the word take,
and an anapest can be created.

Double **take** shakes up
its accented reaction
after the fact.

You see a simply clad lady
standing demurely
before the gilded doors
of the Waldorf-Astoria.

You do a double **take**
as you realize she's
Georgia O-Keeffe!

To recoup a loss,
a sort of anapest

is requested, a double **take**
on a ravaging situation.

Could what appears
to be egregious
lead to a perception
of deeper meaning?

A bleached ram skull
with twisted horns, tossed
into an endless southwest sky,

to im**ply** even **death**
can be **seen** to re**deem**.

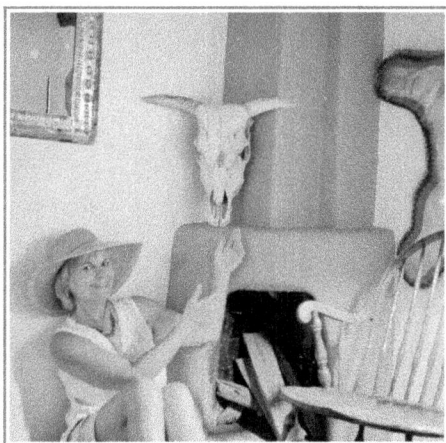

A visit to Ghost Ranch

Day 88

Cautious - Despite - Sagacity

My opa taught me
to be cautious.

Overly so. Could be.

The caution needed
for crossing streets
at the tender age of three
doesn't necessarily
continue to serve me.

Then again, I narrowly
avoided being fatally hit
by two cars illegally racing
on a residential street yesterday.

Despite some sagacity,
I'm less savvy than I ought to be
as to the ways of this new age,
fueled as it is by relentless speed
and ubiquitous insta-blather.

Call me old-fashioned.
I still prefer a slower world,
with space and time enough
to live with a modicum of grace.

Day 89

Cockeyed - Gladsome - Regale

Call me a cockeyed optimist,
or a sentimental fool, if you will.

I'm letting my old-school heart fill
with a cornucopia of gladsome tidings.

There's still enough beauty in life
to regale my soul to its pure delight.

Always with camera in hand

Day 90

Spunk - Grit - Fireball

Spunk!

Sure, I've got that!

Not in the Ferrari
caliber category.

I'm more of a
Deux Chevaux!

On the strength
of two horses,
I make things happen,
create joy in my day.

Grit!

I've needed it!

Life hasn't handed me
a dance card filled
with happy music.

Too many dark tangos
by Astor Piazzolla,

plus a carousel
filled with whirling
Johann Strauss waltzes.

I'll take a slow rhumba, please,
or a gentle bossa nova
by Antonio Carlos Jobim.

That will perfectly suit me.

I've diligently persevered
through several major surgeries
and many deeper woundings.

Fireball!

No. I'm not that.

I've never been able
to handle that level
of high octane,
pedal to the metal.

I'm not a rocket.

On the plus side,
I'm no meteor either.

I'm a steady state
marathon runner,

pumping along
one determined foot
in front of the other.

To mix my metaphors,

I'll still be here tomorrow
tilling my field of dreams.

Posing with a Citroén, Deux Chevaux

About the Author

Eve West Bessier is an award-winning writer. Her work is widely published in anthologies and journals, including most recently the *Los Angeles Review*. She is a monthly columnist for *Southwest Word Fiesta*, and a regular contributor to the *Journal of Radical Wonder*. Eve is Poet Laureate Emerita of Silver City, New Mexico; and of Davis, California. Born in the Netherlands, Eve immigrated to San Francisco at age seven with her mom. She holds a Bachelor of Arts in Creative Writing and a Master of Education. Eve is a retired social scientist and educator. She is a studio musician, jazz vocalist, voice coach, and life coach. She performs her unique blend of vocal jazz and original poetry at conferences, art galleries, and other venues. You can hear her recordings and watch her videos on her website.

www.jazzpoeteve.com

www.ingramcontent.com/pod-product-compliance
Lightning Source LLC
Chambersburg PA
CBHW071215090426
42736CB00014B/2841